Welcome aboard *Glenlee*

We hope this guidebook will help you to enjoy your visit to *Glenlee* and understand more about this historic ship. She is the last of the old 'Windjammers' still afloat in a British port and one of the five great Clyde-built sailing ships left in the world. She is of great importance not only to Glasgow and the River Clyde, but to the whole maritime trading history of the United Kingdom.

The book explains how the *Glenlee* was built, the work she carried out as a British merchant ship, the men who sailed her, and the cargoes she carried. The *Glenlee* story is one of hard work, frequent danger, and constant challenge. Based on contemporary accounts, including ship's logs, our guide tries to recapture the era of sail and Tall Ships.

Most of the windjammers which survived the First World War were lost or broken up in the 1920s and 1930s. The life of the *Glenlee* was extended by changes of use. In 1919 she was sold to an Italian company for short voyages in the Mediterranean. In 1921 she was sold to the Spanish Navy who used her until 1979 in various training roles. In 1992 she was bought by the Clyde Maritime Trust for restoration and use as a maritime museum.

Since 1999 The Tall Ship has become a much-loved landmark and visitor attraction on the Clyde. We hope that you enjoy your visit and that the ship has many more useful years ahead of her.

Contents

Cover illustration by Gordon Bauwens 2011

Facts and Figures

Key dates

1896	*Glenlee* is launched at Port Glasgow on the River Clyde, 3rd December
1899	Ship is renamed *Islamount* and continues her global cargo carrying career
1902	She completes the first of four circumnavigations under the British Merchant flag
1919	*Islamount*'s last voyage as a British cargo carrier. Sold to an Italian company, and becomes *Clarastella*
1922	The Spanish Navy converts the ship to a sail-training vessel and renames her *Galatea*
1936	Outbreak of Spanish Civil War, ship arrives safely at her naval base in Ferrol, Spain
1959	*Galatea* completes her last sea-going voyage under the Spanish Flag
1992	The Clyde Maritime Trust buys *Galatea* and she is returned to the Clyde
1999	*Glenlee* opens to the public after initial restoration
2011	*Glenlee* is towed to her current berth at the Riverside Museum

Particulars	Imperial	Metric
Length between posts	245½ feet	74.4m
Beam	37½ feet	11.4m
Depth	22½ feet	6.8m
Gross tonnage	1,613 tons	-
Net tonnage	1,488 tons	-
Cargo capacity	2,600 tons	-

Amazing Facts

- *Glenlee* sailed completely around the world four times, surviving many storms
- Her main mast is as high as 10 double decker buses placed on top of one another
- Her figurehead is nicknamed 'Marydoll'
- She has been many things, a cargo ship, a training ship and now, a museum ship
- Her nineteen sails could cover a third of a football pitch
- She is the only large Clyde-built sailing ship still afloat in the UK
- Her longest voyage was 1269 days, from 18 March 1916 until 20 October 1919
- She braved the notorious Cape Horn fifteen times
- 25 men crewed her as a cargo vessel compared to over 306 as Spanish training vessel

Glenlee *as* Galatea, *generously donated by the artist Nunez Segura in 2011, for public display onboard the ship.*

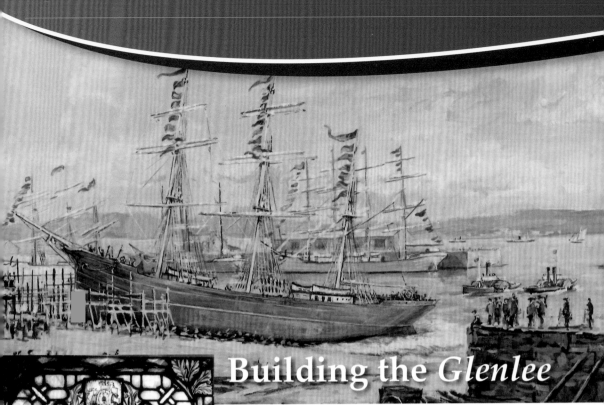

Building the *Glenlee*

Top: Launch of the
Glenlee, *1896. Painting*
by Robin Millar, 1996.

Above: Anderson Rodger
memorial window in the present
Ardgowan Hospice, Greenock

The *Glenlee* is a very special ship for Glasgow and the Clyde. Built in 1896 by Anderson Rodger in the Bay Yard at Port Glasgow, she was the twenty-sixth of 120 vessels built by Rodger between 1891 and 1909, including seven full-rigged ships and three barques. She is the only big Clyde-built sailing ship still afloat in UK waters.

The *Glenlee* is a 245.5 feet (74.4 m) long, steel, three-masted barque with a standard hull, following the design of another vessel, built earlier in the year by Rodger, but with a novel arrangement of masts and rigging known as a bald-headed rig. The steel masts were lower than a traditional rig, but the yards were longer, allowing a large area of sail to be set and operated with great efficiency.

Her construction came at the high point of wind-driven cargo ships. Built to carry bulk loads cheaply, rather than for speed of delivery, she reflected many refinements in design and technology. Constructed piece-by-piece, on keel blocks in an open-air slipway, she was known only by her Yard Number of 324 for six months in the summer of 1896.

The Chief Draughtsman produced plans and working drawings, representing the shape of the ship. Draughtsmen prepared plans for the steelwork, outfitting, masting and rigging. Work then moved into the mould loft, where a full size plan of the ship was drawn, from which templates were made. Many skilled men worked in assembling Number 324, including riveters, blacksmiths, shipwrights, carpenters, painters and riggers, as well as labourers.

The bar keel, the backbone of the ship, was the first part to be laid down. The ribs and deck beams were then erected piece by piece. Over this skeleton structure the steel plates were riveted. Steelwork came from the Lanarkshire Steel Company, whose marks can still be seen on some of the beams. The chart house, deck houses and cargo hatches were all built on the deck beams, before the wooden deck was laid, using pitch pine, 5 x 4 inches in cross section. The three masts, bowsprit, and standing rigging were fitted last, the hull being coated with red lead oxide paint, a material we would not be allowed to use today, to be followed by her final livery and an underwater anti-fouling treatment.

Ribs at the stern of Glenlee *undergoing restoration*

On 3 December 1896, Number 324, now named *Glenlee*, was launched, slipping sweetly and surely down the ways, coated with soap and tallow, to be floated to a fitting-out berth ready for the finishing trades to do their work. In just ten days, the rigging was completed, the finishing touches were made to the accommodation and the various anchors, winches, windlasses, compass and other equipment were installed. A full suit of nineteen sails was also fitted, amounting to some 25,000 square feet (2,315 m²), or more than a third of a football pitch, of canvas.

On 11 December, *Glenlee* was awarded a certificate of registry. Two days later, she set sail for Liverpool. In trials en route, on the Lower Firth of Clyde, she achieved 8 knots despite testing, blustery weather. She was now ready to take on board her first commercial cargo, destined for Portland, Oregon. Her long working life had begun.

Bay Shipyard and dry dock, Port Glasgow c.1900

Final survey document for Glenlee, *December 1896*

Date of completion of Report *Dec 16th 1896*   Received at London Office THUR 17 DEC 1896

Survey held at *Port Glasgow*   Date of First Survey: *15th June*   Last Survey *12th December 1891*

In the *Steel Barque*   *Glenlee*   Rig *Barque*

Tonnage under Tonnage Deck *1515·25*   Master *C. Morrison.*

of Poop *59·34*   Year of Appointment

Forecastle *7·46*   Built at *Port Glasgow*

Bridge House   Half Breadth (moulded) *18·66*   When built *1896*   Launched *3rd Decr*

Forecastle *9·08*   Depth from upper part of Keel to top of Upper Deck Beams *24·80*   By whom built *A. Rodger & Co.*

Houses on Deck *28·20*   Girth of Half Midship Frame (as per Rule) *39·80*   Owners *Sterling & Co.*

excess of Hatchways   1st Number *83·26*   Managers

Tonnage *1613·36*   Length *232·50*   Residence *Glasgow.*

Crew Space *58·74*   2nd Number *19357·95*

Tonnage for Fees *1554·57*   Proportions—Breadth to Length *6·22*   Port belonging to *Port Glasgow*

Navigation spaces *66·49*   Depths to Length—Upper Deck to top of Keel *9·37*   and

Register Tonnage *1488·08*   Destined Voyage *Portland Oregon*   If Surveyed while Building, Afloat, or in Dry Dock.

ONE OR TWO DECKED VESSEL.

CLASS ✠ 100 A1 'Steel'

	Feet.	Inches.		Feet.	Inches.		Feet.	Inches.	
LENGTH on deck as per rule	232	6	BREADTH—Moulded	37	4	DEPTH—Top of Floors to Upper Deck Beams	22	9	No. of Decks with No. of Tiers of Beams

Dimensions of Ship per Register, Length, *245·5* breadth, *37·5* depth, *22·5*.   Moulded depth, ft. *24* in. *1*   Round up of B

5,000 days under sail

*The Tall Ship under sail
by D. McCarroll*

*Master Certificate for William
Fraser, March 1884*

Islamount with James Paterson
tug, arriving Melbourne, 1916

Glenlee left Liverpool on 21 January 1897 under the command of Captain Charles Morrison, born on Islay in the Hebrides, with a crew of twenty-six and a general cargo, for her first commercial voyage. Her registered owner was Archibald Sterling & Co. (also known as the Glen Shipping Company), of Port Glasgow and the largest shareholder was her builder, Anderson Rodger.

This was the first of fifteen long trading voyages round the world, including four circumnavigations and fifteen passages braving the storms and desolation of Cape Horn. She now had an official Lloyds Register Number, 102574, an internationally recognised signal, PMVL, and a registered tonnage listed as 1,613 tons gross and 1,488 tons net.

In March 1898, *Glenlee* was sold to Robert Ferguson & Co. Ltd. of Dundee, and in September 1899 she was renamed *Islamount*. Captain William Fraser, from Montrose in Fife, commanded five voyages for Ferguson, from 1898 until 1904. It was, typically, a period of hard work and fraught with danger, in British waters as well as foreign oceans. In 1900, for example, she not only dragged her anchors at Holyhead, and was in danger of going on the rocks, but, in the same month, a tug on the Mersey dragged her across the pier at Ellesmere Port damaging her bow. The next year, another tug pulled her onto the mud so hard that it took a further five tugs to set her free.

Captain George Bevan, from Liverpool, sailed for one voyage in 1904, from Barking Buoys, London, to Wallaroo in South Australia, loaded with general cargo, and back to Liverpool, in August 1905, carrying wheat. He had difficulty with the crew when leaving Australia and had to hire ten men from the shore to boost crew numbers until they cleared the port. Off the Cape of Good Hope, Edward Kelly, a young English seaman was washed overboard and lost.

Robert Thomas, a Welsh ship-owner based in Liverpool, took over *Islamount* in October 1905 and operated her for the next thirteen years. The close links with Wales were further strengthened under Captain Richard Owens, from Nevin in Caernarvon, who commanded the ship until April 1916, becoming the ship's longest serving master. A month later, another Welshman, David George, from Dinas Cross in Pembrokeshire, assumed command of the longest of all *Islamount's*

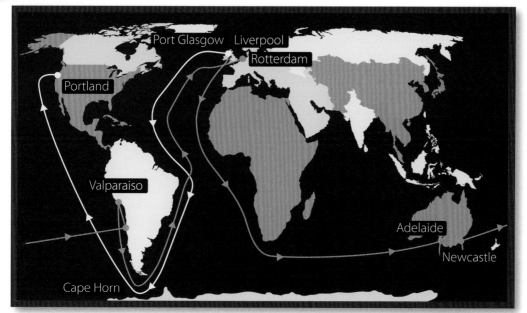

voyages, from May 1916 until October 1919. Like so many others, he saw very little of home during his long career at sea.

In February 1917, leaving Port Phillip, Melbourne, *Islamount*, loaded to the Plimsoll Line with wheat, was nearly lost when the cable from the tug *James Patterson*, parted during the tow through the narrow South Channel, and the ship was in danger of going aground. It took three attempts to pass a new line before she could be towed to safety and the open sea.

During the First World War the Ministry of Shipping requisitioned virtually all British merchant ships. *Islamount* was no exception and was taken over by the Shipping Controller in early 1918 and run on behalf of the government by John Stewart & Co. Ltd., London.

Under the British flag, *Islamount* often endured heavy weather and sometimes suffered severe damage. She lost men overboard in bad seas, and others to illness. On her last voyage, many of the crew, including the Captain, were incapacitated by illness. Life and work aboard was hard, demanding, uncertain and often exhausting, but, right up till 1919, the ship and the skilled men who sailed her helped to keep open the trading routes of the world – and consistently made a profit for her owners.

Maiden Voyage, Jan 1897–Feb 1898, 369 days, under Captain Charles Morrison

First Circumnavigation, Aug 1901–Oct 1902, 285 days, under Captain William Fraser

The Rodger-Sterling Fleet
Glenard (1893) Broken up at Sunderland, 1925
Glenbank (1893) Wrecked off coast W. Australia, 1911
Glenclune (1894) Wrecked off Brazilian coast, 1895
Glendoon (1894) Sunk by U-Boat, 1916
Glenelvan (1895) Wrecked off Madeira, 1926
Glenfinart (1895) Wrecked off Chilean coast, 1905
Glengowan (1895) Destroyed by fire on maiden voyage, 1895
Glenholm (1896) Sunk by U-Boat off SW Ireland, 1915
Glenlee (1896) Restored by Clyde Maritime Trust, 1993–99
Glenpark (1897) Wrecked off South Australia, 1901

Trading under the 'Red Duster'

When *Glenlee* was launched in 1896, Great Britain was known as the 'workshop of the world' and played a major part in the global economy. Vast amounts of raw materials were needed to manufacture goods in Europe and North America and the finished products were shipped worldwide. The British merchant fleet, sailing under the Red Ensign, or the 'Red Duster', was the biggest in the world, and twenty five per cent of the world's trade passed through British ports. Sailing ships like the *Glenlee* still had an important role in the intercontinental trade in bulk cargoes of raw materials at the end of the nineteenth century and until the end of the First World War.

Steamships already carried a growing proportion of this trade, but they were costly to build and required coal and additional men to operate them. Sailing ships were cheaper to build, could be manned with a small crew, often less than thirty men, and, because they used the wind for 'fuel', had an enormous range. *Glenlee* and similar ships were built specifically for carrying bulk cargoes over long distances at relatively cheap rates. *Glenlee* could carry up to 2,600 tons.

*Crew of the **Glenard**, one of the Rodger-Sterling fleet. Just twenty men and the captain's wife. (San Francisco Maritime National Historical Park)*

In her twenty-three years as a cargo carrier, *Glenlee*, or *Islamount* as she became in 1899, earned a living on this trade. There was money to be made in cargo. In February 1914, voyage 'Number 6', under Captain Owens, sailed from Antwerp to Buenos Aires with general cargo, from Newcastle NSW to Talcahuano with coal, from Tocopilla to Durban with nitrates, and from Rangoon to arrive in Liverpool with rice meal in April 1916. The voyage recorded, in October 1916, a profit of £4,048/13/11d and paid a dividend to her owners of £1,400 in June 1915 and the same again in June 1916.

Islamount loaded general cargoes in Liverpool, the Mersey ports, and London; coal in both south Wales and in New South Wales; wheat in Australia; nitrates and *guano* on the South American west coast; timber and grain on the North American west coast; rice in Rangoon; sugar in the Dutch East Indies; and case oil (crude

petroleum) on the North American east coast.

In discharging cargo, too, *Islamount* visited ports all around the globe, unloading, for example, nitrates in the Low Countries and in Germany; wheat and sugar in France; coal and wheat in Southern Africa; oil in Sydney and Nagasaki; and general cargo in Canada.

In port, the speed of unloading and loading cargo determined when a ship could set sail again. Turnaround time depended on the size and type of cargo and port facilities. Wheat, for example, could be discharged in less than three weeks at Ellesmere Port, on the Mersey, and in only 15 days at Cape Town. Coal took between 13 and 17 days to load in Barry, South Wales. Discharging nitrates at Dunkirk took about 20 days, while, on the South American west coast, loading nitrates from lighters could take between 16 and 21 days.

Loading cargo

1. *Timber & wheat*
2. *Case oil*
3. *Guano & nitrates*
4. *General cargo & coal*
5. *Rice*
6. *Sugar*
7. *Wheat & coal*

It was the duty of agents and cargo brokers to ensure that she remained active, busy, and, above all, profitable, but *Islamount* could suffer the frustration of waiting for cargoes to be arranged and the consequent loss of money. Nearly 60% of her time in port might be spent waiting for brokers to arrange shipments. During one voyage from May 1907 to September 1908, on the west coast of South America, *Islamount* had to spend eight months just waiting for a cargo. Even in European ports, she could lose valuable time waiting to load.

Despite such problems, which were not limited to sailing ships, and despite the hardships and hazards which she and her crew faced, *Islamount*, throughout her long working life could draw on her many advantages. Very nearly her whole volume below decks was given to the carriage of cargo. She needed only a small crew to man her and harnessed prevailing winds to drive her. As *Glenlee*, she remains, today, a monument to the global expansion and dramatic success of Great Britain's maritime trade.

Islamount *awaiting berth, Melbourne, c.1910. (Maritime Museum of Monterey)*

> "Ships do want humouring… if you mean to handle them well, they must have been humoured in the distribution of the weight which you ask them to carry through the good and evil fortune of a passage"
>
> (*Conrad*, The Mirror of the Sea, *Section XIV*)

Top: coal was carried loose on Glenlee *and could catch fire*

Top: safe loading of cargo – the Plimsoll Line on Glenlee's *port side*

Right: shifting boards stop cargo from moving in the hold

Cargo is king!

All good sailing begins with careful stowage. The man in charge of this, on ships like the *Glenlee*, was the Chief Officer, the Mate. Stowage of cargo ensured preservation of the crew, no undue stress on the hull, protection of the cargo, economy of space, and fast turnaround time in port. Each ship would have individual characteristics for loading, and most captains preferred the vessel to be trimmed by the stern, often down between two and eight inches. *Glenlee* seemed to sail best when down by six inches.

Within the cargo hold, shifting boards were inserted between the line of steel pillars, staggered and running down the centre, to provide a temporary partition, preventing excessive lateral movement of the cargo. In February 1919, it took nearly fourteen days to load and distribute evenly nearly 27,000 bags of sugar in the Indonesian port of Samarang, destined for Cette in France.

Cargo had to be carefully loaded to ensure the stability of the ship at sea. When bulky but lighter cargoes, such as wool, were carried it was necessary to carry enough ballast so the ship would sit deep enough in the water. Each cargo presented different difficulties. Apart from the weather, the two greatest dangers a ship faced at sea were fire, and the shifting of cargo making the ship unstable. Case oil, securely stowed, was generally safe – unless the cargo shifted and the metal cases leaked. With this cargo, the crew were, understandably, advised to refrain from smoking, so denied one of their few pleasures aboard.

Coal was another potentially dangerous cargo, capable of shifting, heating, spontaneously combusting, and exploding. The only known case of near mutiny aboard *Islamount* was off the Argentine coast in July 1907, when the cargo of coal started to overheat and the crew refused to proceed. A tug was summoned, the cargo surveyed, and 150 tons were shifted to ventilate the hold and make *Islamount* safe to resume her voyage.

Any cargo loaded loose, in bulk, could shift while at sea. Stowage was all-important for cargoes such as wheat or grain, as they could be especially dangerous in this respect. Safety at sea was improved with the Merchant Shipping Act 1876, also known as the "Plimsoll Act", which instituted draught marks and safe loading lines.

Islamount, fully laden at a cargo quay in South Australia, c.1900 (Gwyn Jones)

South American *guano*, or bird excrement, is a rich source of nitrates and was an important fertilizer in the 19th century. Soft and powdery, it stank of ammonia and caused the bags in which it was loaded to rot and the crew's nostrils to bleed. It was never a popular cargo to take on board, and thorough cleaning of the hold was required before another cargo could be loaded.

After cargo was unloaded, or when no cargo was available, the ship would need to be provided with ballast, to preserve her stability, and, if at sea, to preserve her trim. This could be sand or shingle, mud or rocks, sourced locally. In December 1918, when *Islamount* discharged wheat in Cape Town, over 100 tons of ballast were loaded in four days before sailing for Batavia.

Today, *Glenlee* has about 700 tons of ballast on board. Sections of old railway tracks are stowed in the centre of the cargo hold, and pig iron loaded into gabions, or metal baskets, suspended beneath the decks laid in the cargo hold. Visitors will be glad to know that *guano* is no longer stowed aboard!

Guano advertisement, 1884

The Guano Islands off the west coast of Chile, as they are today (John Reston)

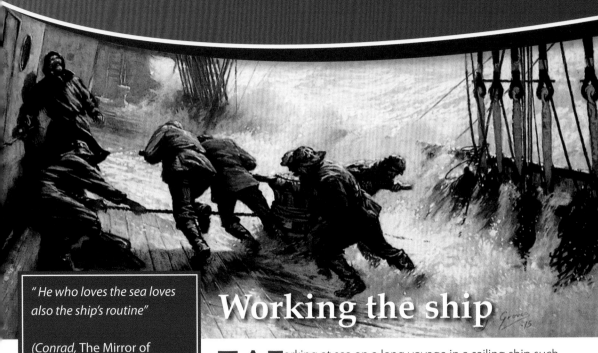

Working the ship

Working the ship

Hoisting the Upper T'Gallant by John Groves

The Glenlee's bell was the ship's clock and marked the change of watches

Working at sea on a long voyage in a sailing ship such as *Glenlee*, whether as cargo carrier or, later, as training vessel, was hard and demanding. It brought its own satisfactions, but was full of uncertainty, unpredictable challenges and constant dangers. Men came from different countries and cultures, with different customs and languages. Nevertheless, all had to be welded into a team to understand the common language and customs of a ship at sea.

The ship's routine was governed by turn and turn about watches, with men working four hours on and four hours off, except for the two, short, two-hour dog watches between 16.00–20.00 hrs each day. As a merchant vessel, the Mate would be in charge of one watch and the Second Mate the other.

The rhythm of this work was also determined by the ever-changing condition of the weather. Sails needed to be set and trimmed, and men sent aloft to loose, reef, or furl sail, whatever the weather. At the same time, the ship had to be steered under the orders of the Officer on watch, decks had to be maintained and kept waterproof, pumps had to be attended to, constant repairs to ship and sails needed to be carried out, men had to be fed – and sometimes cared for when they fell ill or got hurt. At all times the ship needed competent lookouts and helmsmen, while at night, the ships lamps needed to be lit and kept trimmed.

A seaman needed to turn his hand to a multitude of tasks, whether in full daylight or in the darkest night. In port or at sea, the men scrubbed and cleaned decks, sanded metal and wood surfaces before painting, varnishing, or oiling, or tended standing and running rigging. In port, the crew loaded and unloaded ballast or cargo and turned the anchor capstan to raise the anchor when departing. At sea, the rigging capstan, in the waist of the ship, could be needed to haul on a yard brace in heavy weather.

The sailing was often hard, plunging through storms or rounding southern Capes such as the Horn, Good Hope, or Leeuwin, and often there would be little rest for any man aboard. Each man depended on the other for his safety. There could also be many pleasant days, as the ship glided through the Trade Winds at 30 degrees north, or in the southerly South-east Trades, but life in the Doldrums could be frustrating and exhausting as the ship lay becalmed and the crew needed constantly to alter sail to catch any slight breeze, while unceasingly wetting the decks with sea water to stop the wood shrinking.

During all this activity, the Chief Officer or the Mate kept a detailed daily log. This recorded the distances covered, courses, winds, weather, midday position, and also the work carried out by the crew, changes of sail, reports of those ill or incapacitated, and details of loading and discharging cargo and ballast.

After much research, the ship's *Crew Agreements* from 1896 until 1919 have been found, and copied, but only one example of the *Chief Officer's Log*, telling us about life aboard. It is that of Charles Sleggs, detailing the final part of the last voyage of the *Islamount* from Cape Town on the 14 November 1918. She left in ballast to load a cargo of sugar in the Dutch East Indies (now Indonesia), which she delivered to Cette (now Sete, S. France) on the 24 April 1919. The five volumes are kept in the County Records Office, Truro, but a copy is now on display on the ship, providing fascinating reading. In it, Sleggs notes and describes the daily working life of officers and crew as well the tasks, dangers, and regular duties on board. It is testimony to a working life that was tightly structured and endlessly demanding.

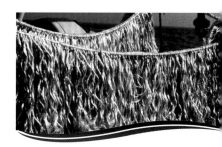

An extract from Chief Officer Sleggs' logbook:
13th August 1919
Strong breeze rough sea spraying heavily, overall cloudy and clear weather. All sails set. Crew employed making new outer jib sheet manilla 16 fathoms 3 1/2" port side. Scraping pump gear. Making bag wrinkle for fore stay. Tradesmen at their trades. Strong NE Trades.

Baggywrinkle being made (E Allen)

S.V. Glenlee

Today, Glenlee's crew use traditional skills to maintain the ship for future generations. (Interpretive Media)

SCALE OF PROVISIONS.

—	Water.	Soft Bread.	Biscuit.	Salt Beef.	Salt Pork.	Preserved Meat.	Fish.	Potatoes.	Dried or Compressed Vegetables.	Peas, Split.	Peas, Green.	Calavances or Haricot Beans.	Flour.	Rice.	Oatmeal.
	qts.	lbs.	lbs.	lbs.	lbs.	lbs.	lb.	lbs.	lb.	pt.	pt.	pt.	lbs.	lb.	oz.
Sunday ..	4	1	—	½	—	¾	—	—	—	—	—	—	½	—	—
Monday ..	4	—	1	—	1	—	—	—	—	—	—	—	—	¼	—
Tuesday ..	4	1	—	1¼	—	—	—	—	—	—	—	—	½	—	4
Wednesday	4	—	1	—	—	¾	—	—	—	—	—	—	½	—	—
Thursday ..	4	1	—	—	1	—	—	—	—	—	—	—	—	¼	—
Friday ..	4	—	1	—	—	¾	¾	—	—	—	—	—	—	—	—
Saturday ..	4	—	1	1¼	—	—	—	—	—	—	—	—	½	—	4
Weekly ..	28	3	4	3	2	2¼	¾	6	½	⅔	⅓	⅓	2	½	8

—	Tea.	Coffee.	Sugar.	Milk, Condensed.	Butter.	Marmalade or Jam.	Syrup or Molasses.	Suet.	Pickles.	Dried Fruits.	Fine Salt.	Mustard.	Pepper.	Curry Powder.	Onions.
	oz.	oz.	lbs.	lb.	lb.	lb.	lb.	oz.	pt.	oz.	oz.	oz.	oz.	oz.	oz.
Sunday ..	—	—	—	—	—	—	—	—	—	—	—	—	—	—	3
Monday ..	—	—	—	—	—	—	—	—	—	—	—	—	—	—	—
Tuesday ..	—	—	—	—	—	—	—	—	—	—	—	—	—	—	—
Wednesday	—	—	—	—	—	—	—	—	—	—	—	—	—	—	—
Thursday ..	—	—	—	—	—	—	—	—	—	—	—	—	—	—	—
Friday ..	—	—	—	—	—	—	—	—	—	—	—	—	—	—	—
Saturday ..	—	—	—	—	—	—	—	—	—	—	—	—	—	—	—
Weekly ..	1¾	4	1¼	⅓	½	1	½	4	½	5	2	¼	¼	¼	3

Daily and weekly food rations for each man were laid out in the Scale of Provisions

Life in the deckhouse

Islamount represented advanced sailing technology, evolved over centuries. Her crew were a self-contained society, a social unit shaped for the specific purpose of running the ship at its highest level of efficiency. Everyone had his place and his role to perform, no one was surplus to requirements, and tensions and differences had to be controlled for the common good. Men from widely different backgrounds and cultures were moulded into a company shaped by experience, long practice, and tradition.

> *"They were a good crowd: sailing ship men, men of the sea who performed their arduous work by instinct rather than by a sense of duty; men who gave their ship a service that was unconditional when she was in need."*
>
> *(Albert Bestic,* Islamount *apprentice, in* Kicking Canvas*)*

The apprentices, for example, their indentures paid for by their parents or other relations, signed on for four years. They, like the crew, lived on the weather decks, shared the men's food, and worked both aloft and below. During this time, they were expected to hand sail, take the helm in fine weather, tally cargo being loaded or discharged in port, and learn the skills of the sea and ships, particularly navigation. Instruction could vary wildly between different masters and officers, but, having served his time, an apprentice would sit for his Second Mate's certificate. This would be the first step in progression to Master, for, in the *Islamount* era, all ship's masters had first to qualify on sailing vessels.

Fred Noonan, 19 years, joined Islamount *in 1913 as an able seaman. In 1937 he disappeared alongside Amelia Earhart whilst navigating their round the world flight attempt.*

The small band of seamen, living in the cramped quarters of the for'd deckhouse, "before the mast", endured either suffocating heat or freezing cold, sunny trade winds or the slashing rain of high latitude storms. Recruited from quayside bars or seamen's hostels, they provided their own clothing, or bought more from the Captain's slop chest out of their wages, and made their own repairs. They worked, divided into two watches – the port watch led by the Mate, and the starboard watch led by the Second Mate. They were on duty, turn and turn about, for four hours, unless weather or sudden crisis kept them on deck.

The sailmaker, cook, carpenter, steward and bosun were known as 'Idlers' because instead of standing watches they worked in twelve hour, daily shifts. Like the crew, their accommodation was on the weather deck and they ate the same food. As tradesmen, the sailmaker and carpenter received higher wages. The sailmaker had a particularly responsible role, caring for sails aloft and stored below. He had to make completely new sails if they were torn to shreds in storms or damaged by chaffing and wear. The carpenter's job concentrated on keeping the decks watertight.

Glenlee's deckhouse as it looks today.

Albert Bestic, holding a monkey, as apprentice onboard the Denbigh Castle. *He later completed his apprenticeship on* Islamount *in 1913 and much later recounted life at sea in* Kicking Canvas, 1957.

The cook was all-important. His skills, or lack of them, could make all the difference on a long, testing voyage. Food and supplies were strictly apportioned. The *Articles of Agreement*, signed by the men on joining, show the *Scale of Provisions* to be allowed and served out to the crew during the voyage. It listed, on a daily/weekly basis, everything from water, biscuits, tea, to curry powder and onions, in addition to lime and lemon juice to prevent scurvy.

Long voyages, often lasting months, provided welcome hours of leisure as well as work. The two dog watches, of two hours each in the late afternoon, provided the opportunity to play music or to sing together, craft model ships, make elaborate plaits and bell ropes, repair clothing and kit, carve scrimshaw, or yarn away the hours with tales of other ships and other lands.

While at sea, this ship's society worked as a coherent whole. Its hours governed by the bell, it was fully fit for purpose. Once in port, the story was very different.

The Cargo Ship
(1896–1919)

Illustrated by Tony Townsend

Masters and men

Sail by John Groves

Above: the captain's Saloon, reconstructed onboard Glenlee *in 2011*

Right: ship's Medical Chest. A variety of concoctions were used to treat ill and wounded men

Islamount at sea was a world of her own, under the direct command of one man, the Master, or Captain. The purpose of every voyage was profit, and its ultimate success depended on the experience and skills of the Captain, supported by his First (or Chief) and Second Officers. The key role was that of First Officer, or Mate, who maintained order aloft among the towering mass of sail and cordage and kept the men fully occupied. He kept his own navigational record and the daily *Chief Officer's Log*.

Surviving records for *Islamount* offer tantalizing glimpses into the daily life of the ship, its crew, their work, and of the challenges a Master had to face. The *Articles of Agreement and Account of Crew*, for example, note details of apprentices, crew signing and discharge, and Consular certificates.

The final voyage of *Islamount*, her longest, clearly reveals the underlying tensions that accompanied order and control on board. Leaving Liverpool in May 1916, the ship's complement was seven apprentices, Master, Mate, Bosun, Ship's Steward, Cook, Carpenter, Sailmaker, three Able Seamen, nine seamen, and one Ordinary Seaman. One apprentice's time elapsed in 1918 and one returned home sick in August 1918. The rest remained for the whole voyage, arriving Cette, October 1919.

Twelve of the original crew deserted in New York between July and August 1916, including the Mate, and had to be replaced. 'Jumping ship' was not unusual. In addition, the Bosun was discharged before sailing; one man was left in New York, ill with dysentery; one able seaman

This is the only known photograph of apprentices onboard Islamount. *Date unknown (Gwyn Jones)*

died at sea; and just three men completed the 41 month voyage to Cette. In all, 77 men signed on over the whole voyage, presenting problems for Captain David George in every port.

Only one *Official Log* of *Islamount*, kept by the captain, is known. It is for a long voyage starting from London, March 1912, ending in Antwerp, November 1913, kept by Captain Richard Owens and countersigned by the Mate, Charles Cowap. Five men deserted from a crew of 37, and two failed to join ship. William Pedvin, aged 36, born in Guernsey, but latterly from London's East End, died on board in September 1913 from 'bronchitis', after seven months of intermittent illness.

This *Official Log* shows continual injury or illness. On 31 August 1912, the Mate fell into the Lower Hold injuring his left arm and left ankle; he was treated "as per the Medical Guide", by Captain Owens, only returning to duty on 23 September. The Log also notes apprentices whose articles have expired, and the attempts by Captain Owens to re-sign them as crew, the attendance of *Islamount* seaman Emil Hagman before the New South Wales law courts – and his later drunkenness at Callao! All reflect the underlying tensions in the crew and the more personal, human demands made of a captain in addition to his business and nautical duties.

Masters and Mates were often at sea for extended periods. If misfortune befell the Captain, then the full responsibility for ship and crew fell on the Chief Officer, who often held a Master's ticket. Chief Officer Charles Sleggs kept the only known example of the daily *Chief Officer's Log* for *Islamount*. It provides fascinating reading.

It starts with letting go the second anchor at Cape Town, 14 November 1918; it ends with mooring "stern on" to the quay at Cette, 9 October 1919. Nineteen days after sailing from Samarang on 28 March 1919, Captain David George and seven other crewmembers became ill with 'Java fever', of which Albert Moginsen died and was buried at sea on 23 April. By the 5 May, the Captain was "very dangerously ill" and only reached hospital in Durban on 18 May.

Sleggs had been in sole charge, tending the sick, and battling fierce storms with depleted crew for nearly two months. Within his five books lies a detailed, gripping, human story, day-by-day, and hour-by-hour, of life and command on *Islamount*. If only we had more such records.

Captain Richard Owens. The longest serving master of Islamount, *from Oct 1905–Apr 1916. (Gwynedd Archives)*

Foreign going

Clarastella at the shipyards in Trieste, 1922. One of only two known photographs at this time

T he end of the era of merchant sailing ships raised questions over the future of *Islamount*. Fortunately, her purchase by an Italian company, and then by the Spanish Navy, secured her active life into the second half of the twentieth century.

Islamount arrived in La Spezia, Italy, on 9 January 1920, the property of the *Societá di Navegazione Stella di Italiana*, based in Milan, and registered in Genoa. There, she was modernised, probably for the Mediterranean trade, and her name changed to *Clarastella*. A new tween deck was installed and twin 220 NHP diesel engines, made by the Italian company Ansaldo San Giorgio of Turin and Genoa, which gave a top speed of 8.5 knots.

Little, apart from this, is known of her time in Italian hands and legends and rumour surround this mysterious period. She probably sailed as far as Tunis, but ended up in Venice on 15 May 1921, and was put up for sale in late 1921. Emilio Casal, an old sailor, interviewed in February 1982 by the newspaper *Faro de Vigo*, suggested that she traded as part of a shady Italian firm, ending up with disputed ownership, but this is hard to verify.

Next news of our vessel is on 14 January 1922, berthed in Trieste, at the Bareino Galleggianti del Cantiere Navale Triestino de Monfalcone shipyard, along with another Clyde-built ship, the *Jordanhill*, (then named *Augustella*). Both vessels were bought by the Royal Spanish Navy for £45,000 and renamed again. The *Jordanhill* became the auxiliary ship *Minerva*, while the *Clarastella* became *Galatea* – suddenly elevated from cargo carrier to prestigious sail training vessel.

Surveyed by Lt. Col. Nicolas Franco Bahamonde, brother of the man later to become General Franco, *Galatea* underwent a major refit starting in April 1922, costing £38,672. Comandante de Frigata D. Ramón Martínez del Moral, the first of twenty-eight Spanish captains to serve on the ship, left Madrid on 20 September 1922, via Paris, to supervise the refit, but this work was fraught with

Galatea en route to Cartagena, still painted in Clarastella colours

Galatea by Nunez Segura

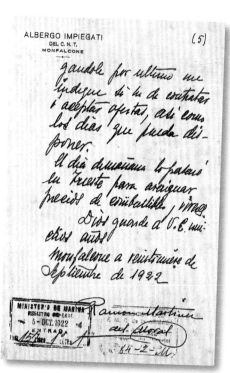

difficulties, including dockyard strikes. He wrote detailed, handwritten letters to the Ministry of the Navy detailing progress and expenses.

The multitude of necessary changes included a new jib boom, enabling *Galatea* to carry 22,500 sq ft of canvas, as well as a flying bridge forward of the mizzen mast. The poop deck was extended and a large deckhouse erected between the fore and main masts. Below the weather deck, accommodation was installed on the tween and lower decks, as well as electrical systems, heating and ventilation, and a chartroom. Galleys, washrooms, new portholes, furnishings and fittings were also provided, to accommodate some 307 men aboard – many more than the twenty-five that often manned her as a cargo vessel!

Finally, on 19 October 1922, Martínez del Moral and a carefully selected complement of 64 men carried out sea trials from Trieste to Brindisi. Teething problems with the new engines meant *Galatea* required further work before sailing for Spain.

The delivery voyage was dramatic and eventful. There were further problems with the engines, and, sailing from Palermo for Cartagena, *Galatea* was caught in a strong northeasterly storm off the Tunisian coast on 11 November. Losing sight and contact with her escorting vessel, *Almirante Lobo*, she was feared lost at sea.

On the 14 December 1922, *Galatea* anchored under the Spanish flag for the first time when she entered Cartagena, where Captain Martinez del Moral recommended further modifications. *Galatea* finally reached her new homeport, the Spanish Naval Base, La Grana, at El Ferrol, on 9 March 1923. She assumed her national number 130 and her call sign became GRVT. Her life as a highly respected ship and pride of the Spanish Navy, had now begun, a life that, today, is still remembered with deep affection by many of those who sailed in her.

Handwritten letter from C.de F. D Ramón Martínez del Moral in Trieste to the Ministry of the Navy, Madrid, reporting on the conversion to sail training vessel, September 1922

Harnessing the wind

Working on the upper yards of a tall ship under full sail is awe-inspiring: no sound of engines, the wind strong behind you, white sails billowing out above and below, the sea breaking under the bows, and a seemingly limitless view to the horizon. It provides immediate, tangible evidence of the incredible fact that wind alone can drive a ship around the world. *Glenlee* originally had no engines: her propulsion came entirely from the nineteen pieces of canvas stitched individually to fit her ten yards, three for'd stays, and mizzen fore and aft rig. The dozens of halliards, sheets, clewlines, buntlines, leechlines, downhauls, and braces were carefully arranged to raise, shorten, and lower the sails to adapt to different wind conditions. Maximum efficiency was the name of the game.

The 'fuel' for a sailing ship was free, but varied in supply, and getting the most out of it to follow a course depended upon the experience, skill, and ability of officers and crew. If the wind came from behind, the ship could sail easily onwards, but if from ahead, the ship needed to tack, or make progress in a zigzag pattern.

When wind or weather conditions changed, or sails were not in use, men had to climb aloft to hand sail. In whatever weather, with men

*"Buque Escuela Galatea"
under full sail*

balanced precariously on footropes high above the decks, the sails had to be raised, furled, and tied securely and neatly onto the top of the yards with short ropes called gaskets.

In a storm, damage to masts, yards, or sails – which might split into tatters with a crack, like an explosion – could very quickly endanger the ship. In October 1946, *Galatea* was practically stripped of her rigging off Punta Delgada in the Azores, and the lower decks flooded, while in a hurricane off New York, in January 1954, no less than seven sails were blown out.

Photographs by E. Allen

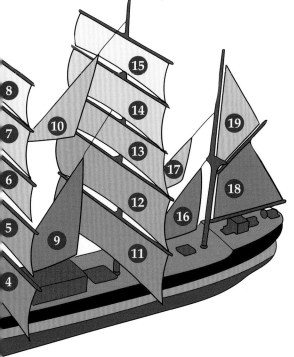

1. Flying jib
2. Outer jib
3. Inner jib
4. Foresail
5. Fore lower topsail
6. Fore upper topsail
7. Fore lower topgallant
8. Fore upper topgallant
9. Tween staysail
10. Tween staysail
11. Mainsail
12. Main lower topsail
13. Main upper topsail
14. Main lower topgallant
15. Main upper topgallant
16. Tween staysail
17. Tween staysail
18. Spanker
19. Gaff topsail

Sail plan illustration by Tony Townsend

Diesel power

The ship arrived in Greenock, 1992 and was inspected at Garvel dry dock

Polar Atlas diesel engines, type M44M, were fitted in 1950

After the First World War, sailing ships became increasingly uneconomical and many were fitted with diesel engines to try and prolong their useful lives. This was true of *Islamount* when she was bought by Italians in 1919 and renamed *Clarastella*. Engines allowed vessels some independence from vagaries of wind. The ship could use power to escape from danger, such as a lee shore, make progress during calms, and manoeuvre under her own power entering port. Dates of landfall could now be more certain, but such ships never carried enough fuel for long ocean voyages.

Italian owners installed the first engines and two propellers in 1920. These were twin diesels, each eight cylinder, four stroke models, which produced 220 NHP and could power the ship at 8.5 knots. To supply them, fuel tanks holding forty-six tons of fuel were also fitted.

In 1925, the Spanish Navy replaced the generators installed by the Italians to provide electricity. La Electricidad Sabadell, a Spanish firm, made the new 100 KW dynamos that provided 120v and 834 amps at 300 rpm. Diesel engines to drive the generators were also installed. These were four stroke, three

Galatea's *main diesel engines before restoration*

Glenlee's *rudder and draught marks during dry docking in 2011*

cylinder models producing 160 BHP, made by Ruston and Hornsby Ltd., Lincoln. This equipment powered heating, lighting, and ventilation, and also the bilge pumps, lighting circuits, radio transmitter, and a servomotor connected to the ship's rudder. One engine and generator remain on the starboard side of *Glenlee*.

A substantial refit under the Spanish in 1950 replaced the ship's main engines with more powerful twin Polar Atlas diesels, Type M44M, manufactured by Aktiebolaget in Stockholm. Each produced 640 BHP at 250rpm. These two stroke, four cylinder marine engines, each weighing 33 tons, gave better performance and safety for men and vessel. Despite the passage of time, these classic engines have been carefully cleaned of rust and dirt, and re-painted in the engine colours used by the Spanish Navy. These are on display in the Engine Room of *Glenlee*.

Engines, to some people, are not as attractive, or romantic, and certainly not as quiet, as sail: but sail and power worked together over four decades. They supported *Galatea* in an active, rewarding life, while training young men in the arts of the sea and ships.

The pride of Spain

B uque Escuela Galatea, orgullo de la nación – School Ship *Galatea*, pride of the nation" begins the anthem of the ship during her time as part of the Spanish Navy. For the 4,000 officers and men who sailed on her during thirty-seven years at sea, the memories and influence of the ship remained vivid and highly evocative.

The training of young men forged more than seafaring skills and naval tradition: it created bonds of loyalty and lasting affection for *Galatea*. Today the original figurehead still graces the entrance to the La Grana naval base at Ferrol, Galicia, and the wheel is still on display in the museum there. For many, it was a sad day when the ship departed Ferrol, and later, Spain.

Galatea regularly made two or three voyages a year into the Atlantic, during which the young men aboard learned not only the teamwork needed to work the ship, but also the skills required of officers, petty officers, and seamen. Each cruise lasted about three months, during which the ship was manned with 17 officers, 30 petty officers and some 260 ratings.

Life aboard was still a challenge. In October 1946 she was caught in a hurricane force storm departing Punta Delgada, the wind speed indicator went off the scale, and half a ton of oil had to be poured on the waters to try and calm the sea around her. Her rigging was stripped, the engine room was flooded, and the pumps had to operate continuously until she could enter Las Palmas for an extensive refit.

Galatea visited many ports, especially those under Spanish control, but during the Spanish Civil War and later the Second World War voyages were restricted. The Canary Islands, Madeira,

Manning the Yards, Ceuta, May 1951. Alfred Alvarez, top right and his friend next to him, take part in the Saludo a la Voz on Galatea. *Manuel Ortiz Araguez (below) can also be seen standing third in, on the yard below Alvarez.*

Juan Gonzalez-Aller, Midshipman on
Galatea 1946–48 (J. Gonzalez-Aller)

Iberian ports, the Cape Verde Islands, La Güera (Spanish Sahara, now Western Sahara), Santa Isabel (now Malabo) on Fernando Po in the Bight of Biafra (Spanish Guinea, now part of Equatorial Guinea); and Dakar (French West Africa, now Senegal), were some of the various ports. North of her Ferrol base, she visited Portsmouth, Bremen, Hamburg, Liverpool and Dublin – where, as existing records show, she was always warmly welcomed.

In her latter years at sea, Galatea visited more westerly ports as part of her training schedule, and between 1953 and 1959 she criss-crossed the Atlantic seven times. In 1953 she sailed into Puerto Rico and New York after a transatlantic crossing. Her return, in January 1954, was marked by some of the most severe weather she recorded. In a storm of hurricane proportions she lost seven sails, 20 cadets were injured, and she was forced to undergo substantial repairs. One seaman on this voyage remembers having to bale the ship for three days with buckets as she listed dangerously.

In 1955 she again crossed the Atlantic, to visit Recife (NE Brazil); a year later she called in at Puerto Rico; in 1957 she visited Martinique (Windward Islands); and in 1958, Pernambuco (NE Brazil).

In the two voyages during 1959, the last as a seagoing train-ing vessel, she called in at Santa Marta (Colombia), Savannah (E USA), Liverpool, Bahia (Brazil), and Dakar (French West Africa, now Senegal). Men who sailed on her final voyages still remember them vividly and with nostalgia.

From 1944 to 1959, Galatea covered over 181,000 nautical miles, and spent some 2,080 days at sea, a record which deserves to be commemorated.

2nd Corporal Domingo Dominguez-Gomez, 19 years, onboard Galatea, *1948. Domingo, 79 years, visited* Glenlee, *July 2008, he removed his socks and shoes so he could once again feel the deck beneath his feet.*

correos

500
f.c.f.a.

República de Guinea Ecuatorial

Galatea *made numerous visits to West Africa, commemorated in this 1996 stamp*

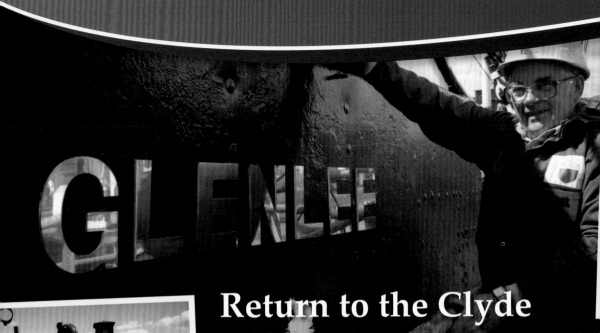

GLENLEE
Return to the Clyde

Top: after much help restoring the ship, Iain MacDonald polishes Glenlee's *name plaque ready for the renaming ceremony, 6 July 1993 (I MacDonald)*

Bottom: laying the opepe weather deck (I MacDonald)

Retired from seagoing in 1959, *Galatea* became a shore-based establishment at Ferrol. She still provided ongoing training for the *Escuela de Maniobras*, where young men learned about rigging and maintenance, and, each year, until 1965, she was given a thorough refit in dry dock. This continued function and attention determined her survival into the end of the twentieth century.

Galatea's Commanders were now directors of the *Pontoon School Galatea*, and her educational role continued until 1979, when she was retired from service. She remained an important and highly regarded feature of the Spanish Navy, as shown by the proposal that she should be a prime exhibit at the prestigious *Expo '92* in Seville. To this end, she was dry docked in 1981, thoroughly re-plated below the waterline, and her masts and yards (which were only replaced in 1957) were taken down and stored, so she could be towed to the Guadalquivir River.

Sadly, at this point in the *Galatea* story, the funding to prepare her for the Exhibition fell through and she could have been scrapped, like many an old, unused, cargo sailing ship. Instead, moored on a remote quay as a storage vessel, she was vandalised, had a seacock removed, and sank. Refloated and pumped out, *Galatea* was moved to the Cement Quay and virtually forgotten.

In 1990, it was realised that she was the *Glenlee*, one of only five Clyde-built sailing vessels remaining afloat, and a naval architect carried out an inspection. The Clyde Maritime Trust had been formed in 1991 to establish a maritime museum in Glasgow. When *Galatea* was put up for sale in 1992, the Trust was persuaded to bid for her. Two bidders took part in the auction but neither could put down cash

Galatea arriving at Garvel Dry Dock, 9 June 1993 (A Miller)

Top left: redundant ballast and cement being removed (I MacDonald)

Top right: stepping the mast, guided by expert rigger, Jamie White (I MacDonald)

Bottom: finally, laying the last plank! (I MacDonald)

to secure the ship. The auction was deferred to the end of June.

This time the Clyde Maritime Trust bid of 8 million *pesetas* (about £40,000) was accepted and *Galatea* was bound for another career. First, she needed some work and a refit before a towing permit could be issued. The Swansea tug *Wallasey* arrived at Seville, and on 1 June 1993, with a riding crew of three, *Galatea* left Spain. She arrived safely in James Watt Dock, Greenock, close to her birthplace at Port Glasgow, at 15.00hrs on the 9 June, some 1,380 sea miles later.

A smart new coat of paint, and the bowsprit refitted in Garvel Dry Dock, and *Galatea* was ready to be towed to No. 3 berth at Yorkhill Quay, Glasgow. On the 6 July 1993, she was renamed *Glenlee* by the Lord Provost of Glasgow, Robert Innes.

A programme of substantial restoration was begun: the aim was to bring her back, as nearly as possible, to her 1896 condition. Unneeded ballast and cement were removed to show the main frames; two new deck houses were installed; skylights, a wheel steering box and grating were made; opepe weather deck laid; Douglas fir tween decks made up; and a replacement figurehead carved and installed at the bow.

While this work was being done on the ship, in the warehouse on the quayside, the masts and yards were being reassembled and standing rigging prepared by specialist riggers. On 16 July 1998, the masts were stepped once more into the hull and by early 1999 the yards and basic rigging were standing 159 feet above the decks and adjacent buildings. *Glenlee* could, once again, hold her head up with pride.

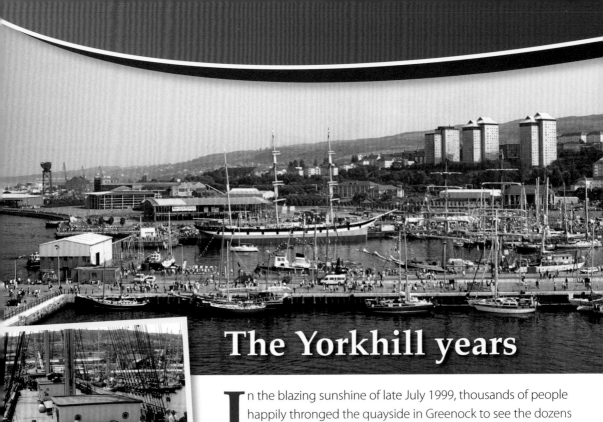

The Yorkhill years

In the blazing sunshine of late July 1999, thousands of people happily thronged the quayside in Greenock to see the dozens of vessels in the Cutty Sark Tall Ships Race. In pride of place was the *Glenlee*, resplendent in her fresh *'ruse de guerre'* paint scheme at Victoria Harbour. During the course of one long weekend, over 10,000 visitors were able, at last, to walk the decks of this remarkable old ship.

This memorable gathering marked a new era in the life of the *Glenlee*, which, on the following 13 August, became the focus of attraction at the newly opened Clyde Maritime Centre on York-hill Quay in the centre of Glasgow. Now, for the first time in over a century, enthusiasts, families, and tourists to Glasgow could see a three masted barque on the upper Clyde and fully appreciate the meaning of 'Clyde-built'.

Although the ship was now open to the public, she still needed investment and further restoration, alongside detailed research into her history. The crew and a willing team of enthusiastic volunteers, many of them skilled shipwrights, engineers, electricians and joiners, all set about further enhancement of *Glenlee*. Their dedicated work, often under adverse conditions, prepared and maintained the ship for the public to enjoy and appreciate.

Over the next twelve years a lot of work was carried out. The cargo hold was opened up and a deck laid, the windlass was stripped and repaired, an education suite fitted out, the poop cabins replicated, the engine room refurbished, and an environmentally friendly heating system installed. Rigging was maintained and extended, the decks caulked and re-caulked, and a lifeboat and a cutter constructed.

Top: Glenlee *takes pride of place at the Cutty Sark Tall Ships Race Greenock, July 1999 (E Allen)*

Bottom: visitors enjoy entertainment on Glenlee's *weather deck (Bill Black)*

A process of maintenance alongside development became the norm, so that visitors from near and far could note progress, as well as appreciate traditional skills employed. Over 350,000 people visited the *Glenlee* at Yorkhill, where they could see caulking, sanding, painting, varnishing, attention to ratlines and shrouds, sanding and cleaning the decks, all taking place as part and parcel of the general maintenance of this historic vessel.

As well as serving as a memorial to the great days of Clyde shipbuilding the *Glenlee* also took on a role as a busy visitor attraction. An educational programme provided workshops and guided tours for schools as well as exhibitions. Lucky children were able to have birthday parties in the tween deck aft, and people could have weddings, parties, and receptions on the ship. With a highly visible presence on the river, the *Glenlee*, known as 'The Tall Ship', became a proud symbol of Glasgow's maritime past.

As part of the regeneration of the Clyde, a new transport museum was built by Glasgow City Council beside the river. In May 2011 at the Council's invitation *Glenlee* moved the short distance downriver to take up her new berth at Pointhouse Quay, where she is 'the jewel in the crown' alongside the Riverside Museum.

Top: Continual maintenance is carried out by Glenlee's *crew*

Bottom: view of the 19th Century Pumphouse building from Glenlee's *fo'c'sle deck, home to the Clyde Maritime Centre, 1999–2011.*

Restoration